Christian Virtues Made Fun and Easy

Grades 3-4

By

Sydney Donahoe

Cover Illustration by

Laura Merer

Published by In Celebration™
an imprint of

McGraw-Hill Children's Publishing

Author: Sydney Donahoe
Editors: Alyson Kieda, Ruth Gray, Linda Triemstra
Cover Illustration: Laura Merer
Inside Illustrations: Becky Radtke

McGraw Hill Children's Publishing

Published by In Celebration™
An imprint of McGraw-Hill Children's Publishing
Copyright © 1999 McGraw-Hill Children's Publishing

Unless otherwise noted, Scripture is taken from the HOLY BIBLE: NEW INTERNATIONAL VERSION®. NIV®. Copyright © 1973, 1978, 1984 by International Bible Society. Used by permission of Zondervan Publishing House.

The "NIV" and "New International Version" trademarks are registered in the United States Patent and Trademark Office by International Bible Society.

Send all inquiries to:
McGraw-Hill Children's Publishing
3195 Wilson Drive NW
Grand Rapids, Michigan 49544

Bible Lessons to Grow By: Christian Virtues Made Fun and Easy—grades 3–4
ISBN: 1-56822-816-3

2 3 4 5 6 7 8 9 PHXBK 08 07 06 05 04

Table of Contents

1.
Count on God to Keep His Promises

Luke 1:26–38; Matthew 1:18–25

Mary was getting married! The wedding, the feast—so much to do! Mary was in a daze. Then, suddenly, Mary was in a dazzle! A bright light blazed before her! She fell on her knees in fear.

To Mary's surprise, a kind voice said, "Don't be afraid, Mary. God has chosen you for something special." Mary peeked through her fingers. She saw an angel! He explained that Mary was going to have a baby. She was to name him Jesus.

Mary said, "B-b-but how can this b-b-be?"

The angel replied, "Don't worry. God's Spirit will cause all this to happen. This child will be the Son of God!"

Mary bowed her head. "I am the Lord's servant. Let it be just as you have told me." Then the angel left.

Mary blinked. She stood up and brushed dust off her clothes. Then she laughed and danced! God promised her a son! And God keeps his promises!

But when Mary shared God's promise with Joseph, he didn't believe it. Nothing like this had ever happened before! It didn't make sense. Sadly, he decided to call off the wedding.

That night, an angel came to Joseph in a dream. The angel repeated God's promise to Mary. When Joseph woke up, he knew that what Mary had said was true. God *had* promised her a son! And God keeps his promises!

Memory Verse

"For God so loved the world that he gave his one and only Son, that whoever believes in him shall not perish but have eternal life" (John 3:16).

Did God Keep His Promise?

Do you know if God kept his promise to Mary? If you do, tell the rest of this story. If you're not sure, read Luke 2:1–20 to find out.

Prayer

Dear God, thank you for keeping your promises. And thank you for your best promise ever—Jesus!

Make a Promise Rainbow

In the Old Testament story of Noah, God put a rainbow in the sky as a promise that he would never flood the earth again. Today, rainbows still remind us that God keeps his promises. Follow the directions below to make your own promise rainbow.

1. Lay a 12-inch sheet of waxed paper on top of several layers of folded newspaper.
2. Choose three or four crayons to use in your rainbow.
3. Sharpen the crayons, using a handheld pencil sharpener or cheese grater. Keep the shavings of each color separate from the others.
4. Spread the shavings of one color into a rainbow shape on your waxed paper.
5. Spread each of the remaining colors next to your first color, also in a rainbow shape.
6. Lay another piece of waxed paper on your rainbow, then cover it with several layers of newspaper.
7. Carry your rainbow *carefully* to an ironing board.
8. With an adult's help, set your iron on a low temperature with no steam. Gently press your "newspaper sandwich" with the iron. Use an up-and-down rather than a side-to-side motion. Lift the newspaper to see if the crayon shavings have melted into a rainbow. If the shavings haven't melted, repeat step 8 until they do.
9. Let your rainbow cool for a few minutes. Then use scissors to cut out your rainbow. Poke a hole at the top of the rainbow and put a string or ribbon through the hole. Hang your rainbow in a window to remind you that God keeps his promises!

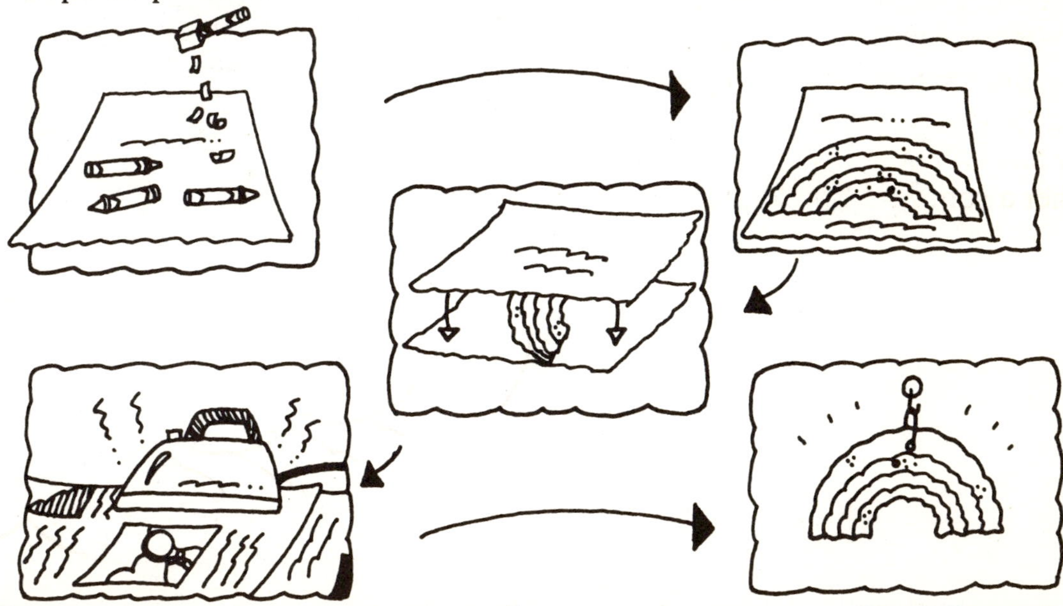

2.
Expect to Be Surprised by God
Luke 2:1–20

Clop, clop, clop. "I'm so tired," thought the little donkey. It had carried Mary for days.

Bump, bump, bump. "This poor donkey has to carry the weight of two," Mary thought. "He's so, so, tired of walking . . . and I'm so, so, tired of riding."

"Mary! I see the town of Bethlehem ahead! Won't be long now!" called Joseph.

Mary prayed, "Dear God, I'm about to give birth to your Son—maybe even tonight! Are you going to surprise me with a nice place to stay in Bethlehem? A place that's fit for the birth of a king?"

Joseph knock, knock, knocked. But all he heard was, "No, no, no. Every room in Bethlehem is taken. We have no place for you."

Joseph felt like crying. How much worse Mary must feel! So he went back to the inn one more time. "Please, please, please," he begged. "My wife is going to give birth tonight. We need a place to stay."

"Oh, all right," said the innkeeper. "You can stay in my stable. But don't disturb the donkeys!"

"A stable? For the Son of God?" Mary asked. "This is a surprise. Oh well, maybe we can make a bed in the hay."

Braaaay, mooooo, whoooo? The stable animals couldn't believe their eyes. A baby born in their barn! They loved him at first sight.

Ah! Oooh! Eeee! Stars exploded in the shepherds' sky! Soaring angel songs lifted the shepherds to their feet. They ran to see the new king who slept under a shining star.

"Ohh. Shh. There now." Mary cradled the tiny child. "Dear God, you did send your Son. He's a wonder. More precious than I ever imagined. You are full of surprises. Jesus is the most wonderful surprise of all."

> **Memory Verse**
> "Today in the town of David a Savior has been born to you; he is Christ the Lord" (Luke 2:11).

Has God Ever Surprised You?
Can you think of a time when God surprised you with something good? Tell someone about your special surprise from God.

Prayer
Dear God, thank you for sending us the greatest surprise ever—Jesus Christ!

Starlight Mint Surprise Cookies

When shepherds walked into a plain-looking stable long ago, they found a surprise inside—Baby Jesus! When you bake these cookies, they'll look plain on the outside, too. But they'll have a surprise inside.

1. Ask an adult to buy a package of premade sugar-cookie dough at the store. Or ask an adult to help you make a recipe of sugar cookies from scratch.
2. Ask the adult also to buy a bag or box of mint-chocolate wafers.
3. Take a "clump" of cookie dough (about 1 tablespoon) and press it around a mint. Place the cookie on a cookie sheet.
4. Repeat step 3 until your cookie sheet is full (leave about 2 inches between cookies).
5. Ask an adult to help you put the cookies in the oven and then take them out when they are done. Follow the directions for baking found in your recipe book or on your cookie dough package.
6. Let the cookies cool, then serve them to your family for dessert. While they enjoy the tasty surprise, tell your family the surprising story of Jesus' birth in a stable.

3.
Spend Time in God's Word
Luke 2:41–52

"Have you seen Jesus?" asked Eli, racing up to Joseph. "I want to show him something."

Joseph replied, "I think he's up ahead."

"Have you seen Jesus, Mary?" asked Anna. "I have some work for him."

"I'm sure he'll be happy to help, Anna. I'll mention it to him."

"Have you seen Jesus, Joseph?" called Uncle Shem. "I want to ask him about something."

"No. If you see him, tell him to check in with me," replied Joseph.

"Have you seen Jesus?" called some children. "We need him for a game."

"No," replied Mary and Joseph at the same time.

"Where is Jesus, Mary?" asked Joseph.

"I thought you knew, Joseph!" Mary and Joseph pulled out of the parade of people returning home after Passover week in Jerusalem.

"I haven't seen him all day. I thought he was with his cousins."

Mary said, "I can't keep track of him and these little ones, too."

"It's getting dark. Should we go back to look for him?" asked Joseph.

"Yes, let's hurry." Mary was already asking friends to care for the younger children while she and Joseph returned to Jerusalem.

No one they passed had seen Jesus. He wasn't at the city gates. He wasn't at his favorite food stall. He wasn't where they had rented a room. Where was he? All at once, Mary said, "I know!" and they rushed to the temple.

They peeked in. Teachers, scribes, and priests clustered around Jesus, who was reading a scroll and reciting Scripture.

Mary ran to Jesus and said, "Son, we were worried. We searched everywhere for you!"

Jesus said, "Didn't you know I needed to spend time in my Father's house?"

Joseph didn't understand. But Mary smiled at her sudden realization. "My son carries God's Word in his heart! Of course, he would be in the temple." Jesus was their son for a little while, but Jesus' true Father directed his path.

As Jesus grew older, God's Word grew in his heart.

> **Memory Verse**
> "I have hidden your word in my heart that I might not sin against you" (Psalm 119:11).

Does God's Word Grow in Your Heart?
Learn a Bible verse. Know a Bible story. Listen to some of the teachings of Jesus. That's how you can get God's Word to grow in your heart!

Prayer
Dear God, thank you for the Bible. Help me always to carry your Word in my heart.

Grow a "God's Word" Garden

Grow in God's Word while you watch this little garden grow.

1. Ask an adult to help you buy a package of radish seeds at the store.
2. Fill a 10-inch flower pot with potting soil.
3. Follow the directions on the radish packet to plant the seeds.
4. Set your "garden" in the sun. Keep the soil moist. It will take your garden a couple of weeks to sprout.
5. Take your Bible with you every day when you check your garden. Use that time to read a verse or two in God's Word.
6. By the time your garden sprouts, God's Word will be sprouting in your heart!

Extra!
Keep reading God's Word and caring for your garden until your radishes are ready to harvest and eat. Just as you produce the radishes for food, God will use his Word in your heart to produce good things, too.

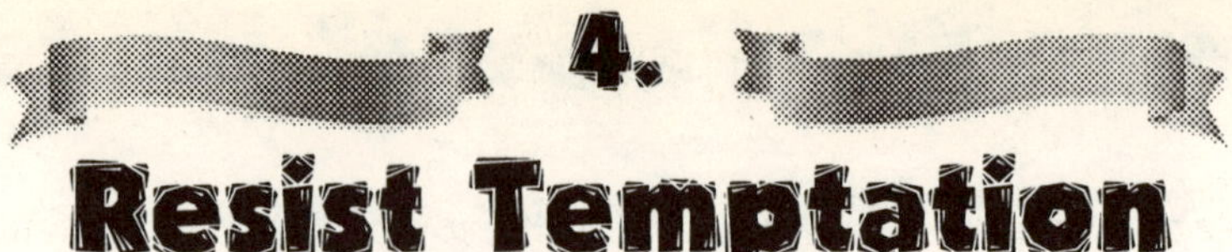

Resist Temptation

Matthew 4:1–11

Right before Jesus began his ministry, God's Holy Spirit called him to spend some time alone. For forty days, Jesus stayed by himself in the desert. During all that time, Jesus didn't eat.

After forty days without food, Jesus was hungry and weak. And guess who paid Jesus a visit right then—Satan! (One of Satan's favorite tricks is to tempt people when they're at their weakest.) Satan said, "I know how hungry you must be. Why don't you turn these stones into bread?"

But Jesus refused. He knew that obedience to God was more important than food. So Satan tried again. He took Jesus to the top of the temple and said, "Throw yourself down. If you are the Son of God, the angels will save you."

Jesus already knew he was the Son of God! He told Satan, "Do not put the Lord your God to the test."

Satan tried once more. He took Jesus to a high place and showed him all the kingdoms of the world. Satan said, "If you worship me, I will give you all that you see."

But Jesus knew who the world really belonged to—God! He commanded, "Satan, get away from me! God's Word says, 'Worship the Lord your God, and serve him only.'"

Suddenly, Satan left. Jesus had resisted Satan's temptation to sin. And do you know what happened next? Angels came and took care of Jesus.

Memory Verse
"Away from me, Satan!" (Matthew 4:10a).

What Would Jesus Do?
When you are faced with temptation, ask yourself this question: What would Jesus do? To remind yourself of this helpful question, print the following letters on a cloth bracelet, a banner in your room, or the front of your school notebook:

WWJD?

The letters stand for What Would Jesus Do?

Prayer
Dear Jesus, help me recognize and turn away from temptation.

Make a Temptation Log

For one week, keep track of temptations that come your way. Every day, write down any temptations you faced and how you handled them.

Temptation Log

	What temptations did you face?	How did you handle them?
Sunday		
Monday		
Tuesday		
Wednesday		
Thursday		
Friday		
Saturday		

5.
Trust God with Your Future

John 3:1–21

Jesus stepped outside into Jerusalem's cool night air. "Psst," a noise came from the bushes at the edge of the porch.

"What can I do for you, Nicodemus?"

"See—that's exactly what I mean! You know everything! This night is black as squid's ink, yet you knew it was me, Nicodemus, hiding in the bushes! You're always doing miracles that prove you're the Son of God!"

"So tell me, Nicodemus. Why are you in the bushes?" asked Jesus.

"Well, I'm an important person around here, you know. I teach. I'm a judge. People look up to me. I couldn't risk being seen with you! Oops, sorry I said that."

Jesus laughed. "I know what people say, Nicodemus. What can I do for you?"

Nicodemus whispered, "I, uh, well, uh, I want to have this eternal life you're always talking about."

"There's only one way to see the kingdom of God, my friend. You must be born again," said Jesus.

"Say, what? How would I do that? I mean, I'm bigger than my mom now. I don't think she could, ah, you know . . ."

"No, no. Your body doesn't need to be born again, Nicodemus. Your *spirit* must be born again, and that will happen when you believe in me, God's Son. You need to have a change of heart and life. Be eager to serve God. Trust me with your future," said Jesus.

"Trust you with my future? Every day from now on? Hmm. I'll have to think about that," said Nicodemus as he slipped off into the night.

What Do You Think Nicodemus Did?
Do you think Nicodemus trusted Jesus with his future? No one knows for sure. But another story in this book gives a clue.

Prayer
Dear Jesus, thank you that I can trust you completely with my future.

Looking into the Future

God is the only one who knows for sure what's in your future. But you can have fun imagining what kind of future he might have planned for you. Answer the following questions. Then, if you like, share your answers with a friend or family member.

What do you think God might have planned for you . . .

one hour from now? ____

____

____

one week from now? ____

____

____

one month from now? ____

____

____

one year from now? ____

____

____

10 years from now? ____

____

____

20 years from now? ____

____

____

Extra!
If you think you can trust God with your future, put a star next to each of your answers above.

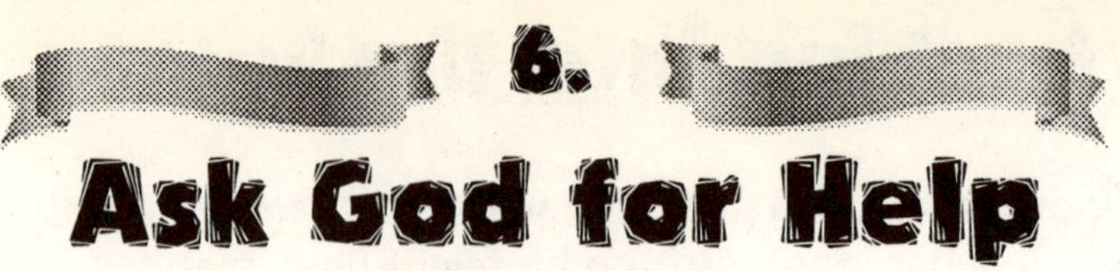

6.

Ask God for Help

John 4:46–54

Push. Bump. Shove. A big man pushed a path through the crowd. He wanted to see the "miracle man."

A young woman slipped through. She wore mourning clothes—someone she loved had died. She was thinking, "If Jesus rests his eyes on me for just a moment, my aching heart will begin to heal."

A group of girls made way for a little boy crying from an earache.

Suddenly, a horse and chariot skidded up in a cloud of dust. A man leaped out and raced to the edge of the crowd. He wore the emblem of the king on his clothes. "Jesus!" he called. "I need your help now!"

Jesus was holding a limp baby girl who was burning with fever.

"Jesus!" called the impatient man. "Please come! My son is dying!"

Jesus looked into the hearts of the people around him. They had come because they knew he would heal them.

Jesus looked into the heart of the man at the edge of the crowd. He didn't believe in Jesus, but he had come anyway. Jesus said, "You will only believe if you see miracles."

"Please! I beg you! My child is dying," the man pleaded.

Jesus said, "You can go now. Your son will live."

Instantly, the man jumped into his chariot and roared off. He knew—he just knew—Jesus had spoken the truth!

Jesus touched the forehead of the feverish baby girl he was holding. She started to coo and gurgle and wave her arms! Jesus handed the baby back to her mother and turned to the little boy with the earache.

The next day, the man was still on his way home, driving at top speed. His servants met him on the road. "He lives!" they called. "Your son lives! He got better yesterday morning!"

The man fell to his knees. "That was exactly when Jesus said my son would live! Praise God!"

That day, the man and all who lived in his house believed in Jesus.

Memory Verse
"The LORD is good, a refuge in times of trouble. He cares for those who trust in him" (Nahum 1:7).

Why Was the Man Desperate for Jesus' Help?
Put yourself in the sandals of the man in the chariot. Why do you think he was desperate for Jesus to help him?

Prayer
Dear Jesus, thank you that I can call on you in times of trouble.

Ask Others About Asking for Help

Ask three friends or family members about their prayer lives. Use the questions below to interview them. Notice that there's a fourth person to interview, too—that's you!

Interview #1 with ____
(fill in the name)

Can you name a specific time when you asked God for help? ________________

____

What happened? ____

____

Interview #2 with ____
(fill in the name)

Can you think of a time when you asked God for help? ________________

____

What happened? ____

____

Interview #3 with ____
(fill in the name)

Can you think of a time when you asked God for help? ________________

____

What happened? ____

____

Interview #4 with YOU!

Have you ever asked God for help? When? ________________________________

____

What happened? ____

____

7.
Build Your Life on Jesus' Teachings
Matthew 7:24–27

Hammer! Bang! Ouch! "Sara, bring me a rag! I hit my thumb again, and it's bleeding," called Caleb.

"Are you sure you want to build our house up on this rock?" asked Sara, as she tied a clean rag around Caleb's thumb. "It's such hard work!"

"Now, Sara. I want you to be safe in this house. I want it to stand up to the storms. When the rivers rise, we'll be high and dry!" Caleb picked up another timber for the foundation.

"I'm sure you're right, Caleb dear," Sara said with a smile.

Hammer! Bang! Ouch! "Sara, I need another rag!" called Caleb.

Swish. Swoosh. Splash. "I'm so glad we're building on the beach, Rebekah," said Gomer. "I'll have this house up in no time. Sand is so easy to build on."

"I love it here, too, Gomer," replied Rebekah. "But I wonder if this will be a good spot when the storms come."

"Ah! Don't worry. I'm pushing these foundation timbers way down into the sand. Nothing will knock this house down!" Gomer went for a quick swim, then back to work.

Flashing lightning! Crashing thunder! Pouring rain! Swirling floods!

Boom! Bam! Crash! "What was that?" asked Sara. "Did lightning hit something?"

Caleb added a log to the fire. "Maybe the storm uprooted another tree."

"I hope it wasn't that beach house falling into the sea!" Sara peeked out the door.

Caleb pulled his mat closer to the fire. "I hope not. I'm just thankful we built our house on solid rock."

Memory Verse
"Therefore everyone who hears these words of mine and puts them into practice is like a wise man who built his house on the rock" (Matthew 7:24).

What Was Jesus Trying to Say?
Jesus told this story for a reason. What do you think he wanted people to understand?

Prayer
Dear God, help me to build my life on the rock, and on you, my firm foundation.

Build Your House on God's Rock

Look at the rock below. Color all the spaces marked with dots to discover the name of God's "rock." Then use crayons or markers to "build" a house on the rock.

Trust God with Everyday Worries

Luke 12:22–34

A man, consumed by worry, rushed past Jesus.

"Stop," said Jesus. "Sit down for a minute. Take a deep breath. Stop worrying!"

"Hah! Don't worry? I've heard that one before!"

Jesus went on in a quiet, calm voice. "Don't worry about what you're going to wear or what you're going to eat. Life is more than food and clothes."

Jesus gestured toward a raven. "Think of the birds! They don't plant crops or harvest seed. They don't store food in barns for the winter!"

"Yeah, well, I don't exactly eat like a bird."

Jesus replied, "God feeds the birds. And *you're* much more important to God than birds!"

Jesus pointed to a lily in the field. "Look at that flower. It doesn't buy clothes. Yet God dresses it in garments more splendid than a king's!"

"A flower? You've got to be kidding."

"What I'm trying to tell you," Jesus explained, "is that you are more important to God than the grass in the field or the birds in the air."

"So, does God want me to eat seeds and wear flower petals?"

"No, no!" Jesus laughed. Then, with a steady gaze, he said, "God wants you to pay attention to the important things in life. Be different from other people—trust God with your everyday worries."

"Oh, I think I get it now. But what about the new clothes I just bought?"

"Share them with people who have only rags to wear. That way, you'll build up treasure in heaven," answered Jesus.

"All right! Thanks for the advice, Jesus. Hey, kids, wait up! Could you use some of these cool clothes? I got them at Levi's!"

Memory Verse
"Then Jesus said to his disciples: 'Therefore I tell you, do not worry about your life, what you will eat; or about your body, what you will wear'" (Luke 12:22).

What Should You Worry About?
Now that you've read the story, can you think of anything God *wants* you to worry about?

Prayer
Dear Jesus, please help me to put all my worries into your hands.

Put Your Worries into God's Hands

Do you have any worries? If you do, write your worries on the lines inside the picture of God's hands. Then, whenever you start to worry, remember that you've put your worries into God's hands, and he will take care of you.

9.
Share What You Have

John 6:1-13

Dan was going to see Jesus—all by himself! Baby Jo was sick, so Mama had to stay home. "Well," Dan thought, "at least I won't get lost! I'll just follow this big crowd." By noon, Dan was sitting in prickly meadow grass under the hot sun. "Wish I could see Jesus better," he thought.

Then Jesus began talking. Dan's eyes opened wide. "Jesus is so far away, but when he talks, I can hear every word! It's like he's talking just to me."

After a few hours, Dan's stomach growled. He had five little barley loaves and two pickled fish in his lunch. But no one else was eating.

All over the meadow, little ones wiggled and whined. Even the grown-ups were getting cranky! Dan's lunch pouch suddenly felt very heavy in his lap. He glanced up. Jesus was looking his way! Instantly, Dan knew what to do. He scrambled over to one of Jesus' disciples. "Psst," he tugged on the man's robe.

Jesus' disciple looked down. "What is it?" he snapped.

Dan said, "Uh, my mama packed this lunch for me. It isn't much." Brightening, he went on, "But the fish are special, and she baked the bread herself! I could, you know, share it."

"With this crowd? I don't think so!"

Just then Dan heard Jesus say, "Andrew, bring the boy here." Andrew grabbed Dan's arm, and away they went!

Jesus knelt down, looked into Dan's eyes, and said, "Do you have something to share?"

"J-j-just two little fish . . . and five little loaves." Dan's voice cracked as he held out his lunch.

Jesus smiled and took Dan's lunch. He bowed his head. So did Dan. Jesus prayed, "Thank you, Father, for this food and the boy who shared it."

Jesus began to break the bread and put pieces in a basket. Then another basket. Then another! He did the same thing with the fish. Jesus' disciples served everyone in the crowd—more than 5,000 people! Everyone ate their fill. Then the disciples gathered leftovers—12 baskets full!

Andrew sat down by Dan and said, "Well, what do you think?"

Dan replied, "I think, even if you have only a little to share, Jesus can do big things with it!"

Memory Verse
"I am the bread of life. He who comes to me will never go hungry, and he who believes in me will never be thirsty" (John 6:35).

How Would You Have Felt?
Imagine being Dan when he gave his lunch to Jesus. How would you have felt?

Prayer
Dear Jesus, thank you for your blessings in my life. Please help me remember to share with others.

Serve Up a Story

Prepare the following recipes (with an adult's help) for a family dinner. While you and your family enjoy the food, tell the story of Dan's two little fish and five little loaves of bread.

Baked Fish

Ingredients:
cod or other white fish, enough pieces to serve your family
⅓ cup mayonnaise
⅓ cup sour cream
¼ teaspoon salt or seafood seasoning
milk
cracker crumbs

Directions:
1. Arrange the fish pieces in a greased baking dish.
2. Mix the mayonnaise, sour cream, and salt or seasoning together, then spread it on the fish pieces. (Make more if needed.)
3. Sprinkle cracker crumbs on top of the fish.
4. Pour enough milk into the baking dish to cover the bottom.
5. Bake the fish 30–60 minutes, until the fish breaks into "flakes" with a fork.
6. Serve and enjoy!

Blessing Bread

Ingredients:
½ cup butter or margarine
1½ teaspoons parsley flakes
½ teaspoon onion flakes
2 tablespoons Parmesan cheese
1 can refrigerated biscuits (10 biscuits)

Directions:
1. Melt the butter in a glass dish or small saucepan.
2. Mix the parsley flakes, onion flakes, and Parmesan cheese into the butter and let stand for 15 minutes.
3. Stretch and twist a biscuit, then swish it in the butter mixture to coat it on all sides. Place it on a cookie sheet. Repeat with the other biscuits.
4. Bake at 425° for 12–15 minutes.
5. Bless the bread when you serve it!

Believe in Jesus' Power

Luke 8:42b–48

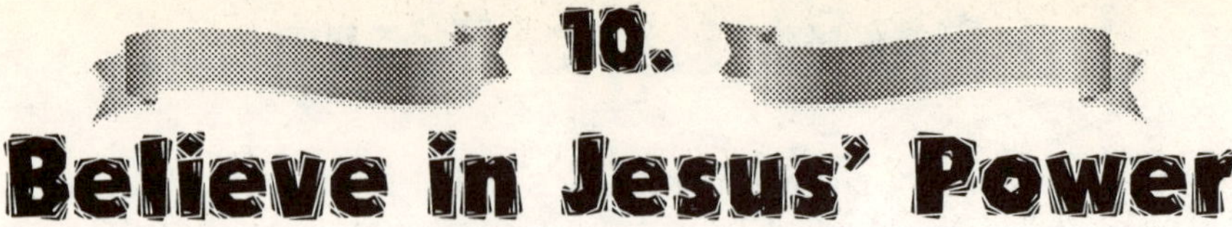

Abigail was taking a terrible risk. She wasn't even supposed to be inside the city gates! Abigail had been sick for twelve long years, and she was supposed to stay away from people until she was well.

But Abigail had heard about Jesus. He was coming to town today! "I have to touch him," Abigail told herself. "If I can just touch him, he'll make me well."

Abigail hurried along the road, trying to look "normal." She'd been sick so long. But today she had to walk, talk, and act like other people. She had to get close to Jesus!

"Oh, no," Abigail thought as she turned a corner. "Look at all these people! I'll never get close enough to touch Jesus!" The crowds pressed in so close that Jesus' disciples were trying to keep him from getting trampled.

"Well," said Abigail to herself, "I'll just have to squeeze in." Abigail ducked her head and pushed into the crowd with her hand stretched out.

"Oof, whew!" It didn't take long for Abigail to get winded. She was weak, and the crush of the crowd was strong. "I . . . I'm getting dizzy. I think I'm going to faint!" Abigail stumbled and started to fall. Just as she hit the ground, she stretched out her hand as far as she could in one last try to touch Jesus.

Abigail slowly opened her eyes. "Nobody stepped on me!" was her first thought as she sat up. Suddenly, she jumped to her feet. "I'm well!" she called out loud. "I'm well! I'm well!" Then Abigail noticed the crowd wasn't moving. The people were standing still, looking at Jesus.

"Who touched me?" Jesus asked the crowd. No one answered. Abigail was suddenly afraid. She had touched Jesus.

Finally, one of Jesus' disciples said, "Master, all these people are pressing and crowding against you. Many of them touched you."

But Jesus said, "Someone touched me. I felt power going out of me. Who touched me?"

At last, Abigail came forward and fell at Jesus' feet. "It was I, Master. I . . . I knew that if I could touch even the hem of your robe, I would be healed. And I was! The instant I touched you, I was healed!"

Jesus smiled and touched Abigail's bowed head. "Daughter, your faith has healed you. Go in peace."

Abigail stayed on her knees as she watched Jesus begin walking down the road again. "He healed me!" she sang out. "His power healed me!"

Memory Verse
"The LORD on high is mighty" (Psalm 93:4b).

What Made Jesus Notice?
Why do you think Jesus noticed Abigail's touch, when so many other people were crowding around him, too?

Prayer
Dear Jesus, I praise you for your mighty power!

Sing Out a Power Song

Sing the song below, using the hand motions listed (or make up your own). Teach the song to some friends, then give a concert! (The music may be found in music stores and some church songbooks.)

Awesome God*
by Rich Mullins

Our God	*point up*
is an awesome	*hand flat, palm toward face, make circular motions*
God,	*point up*
He reigns	*make rain-falling motions with fingers*
from heaven above	*point up*
with wisdom,	*touch head*
power	*hold left arm out straight, place right hand on inside of left elbow*
and love.	*cross hands over heart*
Our God	*point up*
is an awesome	*hand flat, palm toward face, make circular motions*
God!	*point up*

*©Copyright 1988 Edward Grant, Inc.

Take Time to Care for Others

Luke 10:30–37

Clouds of dust rose from the road as Asher and his donkey walked to Jericho. They had started late. The sun was already sinking in the sky.

"Let's hurry, fella," Asher told his donkey. "Robbers and bad men hide in the cliffs and caves along this road. We've got to get out of here before dark!" But the long shadows cast by the overhanging cliffs spooked the little donkey. He would walk only a few halting steps at a time.

Asher drank a swig of water from his jug and splashed a little on the back of his neck. "Better put this away now," he thought. "In this heat, I'm going to need every drop of water I brought along."

"Hey! Is the sun playing tricks on me?" Asher asked his donkey. (The donkey didn't answer, of course.) "Is that a man or a mirage up ahead?" As they got closer, Asher saw it was a man, slumped by the road, holding his head and groaning.

"Let's take a look at you," Asher said, kneeling down. Through swollen lips, the man explained that robbers had attacked him, took his money, and left him to die.

"Two other men passed by," said the man, "But they didn't stop. Guess they were in a hurry."

Asher gave the man a drink, then used the rest of his water to wet a piece of cloth he'd planned to sell in Jericho. Asher bandaged the man's head and helped him up on the donkey.

"I'll take you to an inn nearby," he said.

This time, the donkey walked quickly and carefully. He seemed to know he carried an important burden.

At the inn, Asher paid for a room for the man and himself, as well as hay for the donkey. The next morning, Asher gave the innkeeper more money. "I'll pay you to take care of the injured man until I return from Jericho. Then I'll help him get home."

The innkeeper looked surprised. "Do you know the guy?" he asked.

Asher replied, "No. I never met him before yesterday. But when God shows me a need, I do what I can to help. It's as simple as that!"

Memory Verse
"The King will reply, 'I tell you the truth, whatever you did for one of the least of these brothers of mine, you did for me'" (Matthew 25:40).

Why Did Asher Help?

Why do you think Asher went out of his way to help the man who had been beaten and robbed?

Prayer

Dear Jesus, please help me to see the needs around me and to help people as if I were helping you.

Act Out the Story

Invite some friends or family members to help act out the story of the Samaritan man who took time to care. Before you begin acting, read the story in Luke 10:30–37 to find out more about the two people who passed by without helping.

Actors
Robbers
Injured man
Two people who passed by without helping
Asher, the man who stopped to help
Donkey
Innkeeper

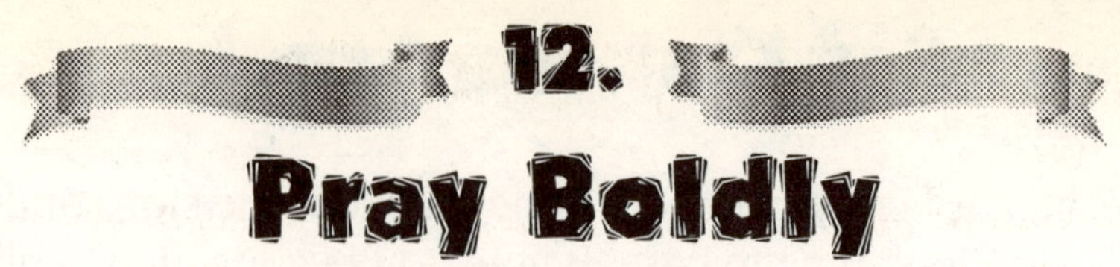

12.
Pray Boldly

Luke 11:1–10; Matthew 6:9–13

It was a sunny spring morning. Jesus and his disciples were praying in a quiet garden. When Jesus finished praying, one of his disciples said, "Lord, teach us to pray. We want to pray the right way."

Jesus smiled. He knew that prayer is simply talking to God. "Well, since you asked," Jesus said, "here's an example of how to pray:

> Our Father, who art in heaven,
>   hallowed be thy name,
>   thy kingdom come,
>   thy will be done,
>   on earth as it is in heaven.
> Give us this day our daily bread;
> and forgive us our trespasses,
>   as we forgive those
>   who trespass against us;
> and lead us not into temptation,
>   but deliver us from evil.
> For thine is the kingdom,
>   and the power, and the glory,
>   forever and ever. Amen

"I'll give you some more advice," Jesus said. "Don't bargain with God. Be bold. Ask him for what you need. To put it simply:

> Ask and you'll receive;
> Seek and you'll find;
> Knock and the door will be opened.

"God loves you! He wants to give you good things," Jesus finished.

Memory Verse
Take some time to memorize the prayer Jesus taught his disciples. As you pray out loud, pretend that Jesus is saying the words with you.

Are These Things in Jesus' Prayer?
Read Jesus' prayer again. See if you can find these parts of the prayer:
- ◆ praise
- ◆ request for daily needs to be met
- ◆ request for forgiveness of sins
- ◆ promise to forgive others
- ◆ request for help not to sin

Prayer
Dear Jesus, I thank you that I can talk to you anytime, and that you will answer my prayers.

Make an "Anytime" Prayer List

You can talk to God in prayer *anytime!* You can say a prayer out loud or just think it in your mind. The tricky part is remembering to pray! Make a list of times when saying a prayer could help you. Then remember to pray at those times! A few ideas are listed below to get you started.

Times when it could help me to say or think a prayer:

1. When I'm taking a test.

2. When I sit down to eat.

3. While I'm doing my homework.

4. ____

5. ____

6. ____

7. ____

8. ____

9. ____

10. ____

11. ____

12. ____

13. ____

14. ____

15. ____

16. ____

17. ____

18. ____

19. ____

20. ____

13.
Remember to Say "Thank You"
Luke 17:11-19

The ten men sitting at the village gate were covered with ugly spots of leprosy. The disease numbed their skin. The men had no feeling in their hands, feet, or faces. They sat and hoped someone would throw some table scraps their way.

Just then Micah, one of the ten lepers, heard footsteps. He peeked out from under the rag that covered his head. "Maybe these travelers will toss us a few coins," he said to the others.

As the travelers came closer, Micah realized that the leader of the group was Jesus. Struggling to his feet, Micah called to the other nine, "Get up! Get up! Jesus is coming. The man who heals!"

The ten lepers limped after Micah, calling, "Jesus! Have pity on us!"

The twelve men with Jesus stopped short at the sight of the lepers. But Jesus came close and looked into the eyes of each man. He said, "Go, show yourselves to the priest."

"To the priest?" wondered Micah. When sick people became well, they were to go to the priest to be pronounced "clean." But lepers never got well.

Even so, Micah turned around and began walking back to the village. "Ouch!" he cried. He looked down at his foot. He'd stepped on a stone, and it had hurt! "I can feel my foot!" he shouted. "The spots are gone, too!"

Suddenly, the ten lepers were shouting, laughing, singing, dancing, and leaping for joy! By the time they got to the priest, all their spots were gone! The lepers raced out of the temple. They were clean! Micah leaped higher than the rest. He could go home to Samaria! He could hold his children and hug his wife.

"Wait. I'm forgetting something!" Micah ran up and down the village streets. Where had those travelers gone? Finally, Micah spotted them getting a drink of water at the village well.

"Praise God! I'm healed! Praise God!" Micah called as he fell to his knees at Jesus' feet. "Thank you, Master! Thank you! You've given me life again!"

Jesus looked around. "Where are the others? Were not all ten cleansed?" Micah didn't know what to say.

Then Jesus took Micah's arm and raised him to his feet. Micah shivered. It was the first time in years that someone had touched him! Jesus said, "On your feet now, friend. Go on home. Your faith has made you well."

Memory Verse
"Give thanks to the LORD, call on his name" (1 Chronicles 16:8a).

What Do You Think Jesus Thought?
When only one man out of ten returned to say thank you, what do you think went through Jesus' mind?

Prayer
Dear Jesus, thank you for the wonderful things you do in my life. Help me to remember to always give thanks to you.

Make Micah Jump for Joy

What do you think Micah looked like? Trace or copy the outline below onto a piece of white paper, then draw in the face and add a beard, hair, and other features to create your "Micah." Next, cut out your figure of Micah. Then, follow the directions to make Micah leap for joy!

1. Obtain the following materials:
   rubber band, craft stick, glue or tape.
2. Attach a rubber band to the back of Micah's head. Leave part of the rubber band free (see illustration).
3. Beginning at the top of Micah's head, glue a craft stick lengthwise to the back of the figure (see illustration). Be sure to place the craft stick so that it cannot be seen from the front of the figure. Let dry.
4. Holding the top of the rubber band, bounce Micah up and down.

14.
If You Make a Mistake, Go to God

Luke 15:11–32

The pigs slurped up their meal. Fig skins, moldy bread, and rotten pea pods sloshed in spoiled milk and animal fat. Yum!

A skinny young man named Elam sat on a rock nearby. His mouth watered while he watched the pigs eat. "Oh, that fat looks delicious! And pea pods! On my father's farm, we didn't even feed pea pods to the pigs—we threw them away! Now I'd eat pea pods in a minute. I'm starving."

Dazed from hunger, Elam remembered the day he had demanded his share of the family's land and livestock. "Give it to me now!" he'd told his father. "I'm going to make a name for myself in the world." The next day, Elam sold his land, cattle, sheep, and goats. So much money! It would last forever! But his new city friends helped him spend it—fast. When the money ran out, his friends ran off. Then a famine came. And now Elam was wishing he could eat pig slop.

"What am I thinking?" Elam said. "I could beg my father to forgive me and let me work as a servant. On my father's farm, even the servants had plenty of food." Elam struggled to his feet and began the long journey home.

Old Shashak enjoyed the evening breeze on his rooftop porch. At the end of a day, he liked to look at his land, buildings, and livestock. But the sweet pleasure in his farm was seasoned with sadness when he glanced at the land his son Elam had sold. The land didn't matter, of course. But oh how Shashak missed his son.

Was that a traveler coming up the road? Could it be? No, this young man was much too thin. Elam was husky and strong. But see that curly black hair that would never lie flat? It was Elam! Shashak nearly flew off the roof in his haste. He ran as soon as his feet hit the ground.

When Elam saw his father running toward him, he fell on his knees in the dirt. "Father, I have sinned against God and against you. I am no longer worthy to be called your son."

"Nonsense!" cried Shashak with a joyful hug. "You're my beloved child, and you've come home!" He called to his servants, "Kill the fattened calf! We're going to have a party! My son who was lost has been found! Elam has come home!"

Memory Verse
"If we confess our sins, he is faithful and just and will forgive us our sins"
(1 John 1:9a).

Why Wasn't Shashak Angry?
Put yourself in Shashak's shoes. Why do you think he was glad instead of mad when his son came home?

Prayer
Dear God, thank you that you always forgive me when I admit I have made a mistake.

Plan a Welcome Home Party

Who in your family could use a welcome home party? Maybe it's a dad who works hard, a sister who needs some cheering up, a mom who takes care of you, or a grandparent who bakes or builds things for you. Choose the guest of honor, then plan a surprise welcome home party.

1. Let the rest of your family know about the party, but keep it a secret from the guest of honor.
2. Ask an adult to help you plan and prepare the guest of honor's favorite meal.
3. Make "Welcome Home" signs for decorations. On the signs, write messages to the guest of honor.
4. Make the guest of honor's place at the table special. Use a pretty plate, colorful napkin, or a placemat you've made. Put some flowers on the table.
5. Get a gift ready ahead of time. Make an art project, write a poem, or give some "gift certificates" for things you could do for the guest of honor.
6. Gather at the door when it's time for the guest of honor to arrive. When the door opens, yell "Surprise! Welcome home!" Escort your guest to the party table.
7. Before dinner, say a prayer thanking God for the guest of honor. As the guest of honor enjoys the food, you and others at the table can say why you're glad he or she is a part of your family.

15.

Remember: Children Are Special to Jesus

Luke 18:15–17

My boo-boo hurts!" wailed three-year-old Rachel.

"Shh," Rachel's mother replied. "We're almost there. See? I'll lift you up high, so you can see Jesus."

"I see him!" Rachel slid down into her mother's arms again. She sniffled. "Will he heal my boo-boo?"

"Yes, I'm sure he will. See all these other children around us? They're going to see Jesus, too. He's kind, and he'll heal all the boo-boos, fevers, tummy aches, and crippled little legs."

"Excuse us, ma'am." Two big men stepped in front of Rachel and her mother. They were stretching a rope through the middle of the crowd. "Sorry, but Jesus can't see any more children today. Come back another time." Children began to whine and cry; mothers began muttering angrily.

A hush fell over the crowd. The two men glanced up, then froze in place. Children stopped fussing. Mothers stopped muttering. Jesus himself stepped up to the rope. "Why the rope, Peter and James?"

"Well . . . you know . . . the meeting we had this morning, and all. You have so many things to do today. Don't you remember?" asked Peter.

"Yeah. We're just doing a little crowd control here," added James. "You can't spend all day with children, you know. You've got important people to see."

Jesus stood silent for a minute. Then he reached across the rope and held out his arms to little Rachel. Her eyes opened wide as she looked into Jesus' face. She smiled as she nestled her head on his shoulder.

Jesus took the rope from Peter and James and dropped it to the ground. "Let the little children come to me," he said. "Don't ever get in their way or make it hard for them. These children are my father's pride and joy."

"B . . . but . . . we don't understand," Peter and James said.

"Look around you. See how these children trust and love me?" Silently, little ones slipped through the crowd to gather around Jesus. They gripped his robe in their little fists, clung to his legs, and clutched his fingers with their warm, soft hands.

Jesus continued, "Now, pay attention. This is the important part: You must have the simple faith of a child to enter God's kingdom." Jesus smiled down at the little crowd around him, then sank into their midst. Rachel looked up from his lap. "I'm all better now. Thank you, Jesus."

Memory Verse
"Let the little children come to me"
(Luke 18:16a).

Why Do Children Love Jesus So Much?
Imagine being part of the group of children who stood around Jesus. Why do you think children love Jesus so much?

Prayer
Dear Jesus, thank you for loving me so much. I love you, too.

Look Who's Special!

Tape or glue several sheets of plain white paper together to make a banner about one yard long. (Or use butcher paper to make a banner.) Write these words on the banner in colorful letters:

Look Who's Special to Jesus!

Decorate the banner with drawings, if you'd like. Then, ask an adult's permission to tape the banner to a bathroom mirror or other mirror. Every time you look into the mirror, you'll see someone who's special to Jesus—you!

16.
Give People a Chance to Change

Luke 19:1-10

Jesus was walking through the city of Jericho. As always, crowds swarmed around him.

One of his disciples whispered, "Are we staying in Jericho tonight, Jesus? Where will we sleep?"

Just then, another disciple ran up. "Jesus! We're almost out of the city gates. We're not camping on Jericho Road tonight, are we? It's dangerous!"

Jesus stopped. He said, "Yes! This is the place!"

"Here? We're camping under this sycamore tree tonight?" asked Jesus' disciples.

"No, no," said Jesus. "We're not staying here. We're just meeting our host here!"

"Oh," said the disciples. They looked around. No one came forward to greet them. "Who is it?" they asked.

"It's Zacchaeus!" Jesus exclaimed. Then he looked up into the sycamore tree and said, "Zacchaeus, you can come down now!"

At first nothing happened. Then the tree branches rustled. A leg dangled down from the tree. Then two legs. The legs were very short. It was still a long drop to the ground. Jesus said to his disciples, "Help our host down from the tree, please."

Mark and Thomas grabbed the man's legs and lowered short little Zacchaeus to the ground. Zacchaeus dusted off his robe, pulled a leaf from his hair, and said, "I will gladly welcome you to my house!"

The people in the crowd started muttering.

"Zacchaeus! Jesus is staying with Zacchaeus? But he's a tax collector! He's mean and stingy, and he cheats us. Jesus is staying with a sinner!"

"Ahem. AHEM!" Zacchaeus cleared his voice and stood as tall as he could. "I would just like to say, Lord . . ." The crowd grew quiet. "I would just like to say that I've decided to change my ways. So, starting here and now, I will give half of all I have to the poor. And if I have cheated anyone, I will pay back four times the amount!"

The crowd cheered!

Jesus hugged Zacchaeus and said, "This is salvation day at your house, Zacchaeus! This is why I came to earth—to find people like you who were lost and bring them back to God."

Memory Verse
"I will give you a new heart and put a new spirit in you" (Ezekiel 36:26a).

How Did Jesus Know?
How do you think Jesus knew Zacchaeus was up in the tree?

Prayer
Dear Jesus, thank you for giving me a chance to have a change of heart. Please help me to give other people the same chance.

A Puppet Show

1. Trace or copy the figures of Jesus and Zacchaeus onto plain white paper. Trace the two circle patterns, too.
2. Glue the two figures and two circles onto stiff white paper (posterboard), then cut around the outside lines.
3. Color the figures and the feet.
4. Poke a small hole in each place marked by an X.
5. Using a metal fastener, attach one set of feet to the back of each of the two figures. Now you have two puppets!
6. Practice "walking" the puppets. Do they walk best on a tabletop, rug, or bed? When you've found a good place to walk your puppets, put on a puppet show for your family, telling the story of Jesus and Zacchaeus.

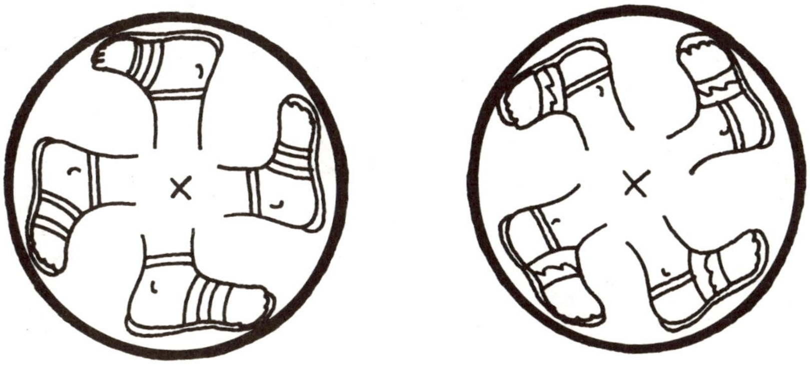

17.
Always Praise the Lord
Matthew 21:8–11

Nate and his big sister Sheerah danced around their dusty yard. They leaped in the air and shouted for joy! Dad was taking them to greet Jesus as he entered the city! The Miracle Man was coming to town! He would be riding on a donkey.

"Dad! Hurry! We're the only ones on our road who haven't left yet!" they called.

"Coming, coming," said Dad, huffing and puffing as he rushed from the backyard. "Had to cut these palm branches first. Here."

Nate and Sheerah grabbed the branches and waved them in the air. With Dad hustling along behind them, they skipped and sang their way down the road.

> "Hosanna!
>   Hosanna!
>   Jesus is sent by God!
> Hosanna!
>   Hosanna!
>   Praise his name in the highest!"

"Here's a good spot, Sheerah!" called Nate. "Can you see Jesus yet, Dad?" (It was a good thing their dad was so tall.)

"Yes! Here he comes! Sing your praise song, kids!" Dad wriggled out of his cloak and spread it out on the dusty road. Other men did the same, making a path fit for a king.

When Sheerah and Nate finally glimpsed Jesus, they laid their palm branches down on top of Dad's cloak. Other kids did, too.

The children sang their praise song, loud and clear. Then Jesus and the donkey passed by right in front of them. For just a moment, the donkey's clip-clop sounded like delicate crystal bells ringing with joy, and the children's sweet, pure praises sounded like angels' songs.

Memory Verse
"Sing praises to God, sing praises; sing praises to our King, sing praises" (Psalm 47:6).

How Do You Think Jesus Felt?
When Jesus rode into Jerusalem and heard the children's song, how do you think he felt?

Prayer
Dear Jesus! I praise your holy name!

Write a Praise Song to Jesus

Jesus loves to hear children sing praises to him! Here are three different ways you can praise Jesus in song.

1. Sing a song you know.
   What's your favorite praise song? Sing it to Jesus! If you don't have a favorite, try this one:

   Hallelu, Hallelu, Hallelu, Hallelujah! Praise ye the Lord.
   Hallelu, Hallelu, Hallelu, Hallelujah! Praise ye the Lord.
   Praise ye the Lord! Hallelujah! Praise ye the Lord, Hallelujah!
   Praise ye the Lord! Hallelujah!
   Praise ye the Lord!

2. Sing new words to a tune you know.
   Try this one, then make up your own songs.
   (To the tune of "The B-I-B-L-E—That's the Book for Me")

   He's J-E-S-U-S—the one who cares for me!
   I pray to him, I sing to him,
   And he takes care of me!

3. Did you like Nate and Sheerah's song? Jesus did! You can make up your own tune and words for a new song to Jesus! Ring bells or add other joyful sounds to your song.

18.
Accept God's Gift to You

John 19:16–20:18

ate and Sheerah kicked the dried-up palm branches on the road. It seemed like ages since they had gaily waved branches like these for Jesus. But it had been only a week. And now, Jesus was dead.

Yesterday was the Sabbath, the day of rest. But it seemed more like a day of sadness. Adults and children all over the city were stunned. Their beloved Miracle Man had been put to death on a cross.

Today was Sunday, the first day of the week. Nate and Sheerah felt they needed to go somewhere or do something. So they walked.

After a while, Sheerah stopped. "Look where we are, Nate," she whispered.

Nate looked around. He saw a steep hill ahead. "It's Golgotha," he said. "It's where Jesus died."

Sheerah grabbed Nate's arm. "I heard Dad tell Mom that two men laid Jesus' body in a tomb near here, then rolled a big stone in front it. Their names were Joseph and Nic . . . nico . . ."

"Nicodemus," said Nate. "Do you think we could find Jesus' tomb? We could say a prayer there."

"Well, let's look around," answered Sheerah. As Sheerah and Nate quietly explored a nearby garden, they heard a woman crying. They peeked around a tree and recognized Mary Magdalene, one of Jesus' best friends.

"She's sad because he's dead," said Sheerah.

"No, look! She's crying because the stone is gone and the tomb is empty!" whispered Nate.

"Someone must have taken Jesus' body." Tears began to roll silently down the children's cheeks.

Just then, a glowing light filled the gloomy garden. Nate and Sheerah saw Mary Magdalene look up at the light. At first she looked afraid. Then her eyes began to sparkle. She leaped to her feet and lifted her hands in the air. Joyfully, Mary whirled in a circle, then left the garden on dancing feet.

Nate and Sheerah felt the air stir as Mary swished past their tree. They heard her laugh and sing, "Jesus is risen! My Lord has risen from the dead!"

"Just like he said!" exclaimed Nate and Sheerah. The light sparkled in their eyes, too, as they raced home to spread the good news.

> **Memory Verse**
> "He is not here; he has risen!" (Luke 24:6a).

Why Did Mary Cry?
When Mary Magdalene saw the empty tomb, why do you think she cried? Read John 20:10–18 to find out why Mary's tears turned to joy.

Prayer
Dear Jesus, thank you for dying and rising from the dead and giving me the gift of eternal life!

Tell Me a Story

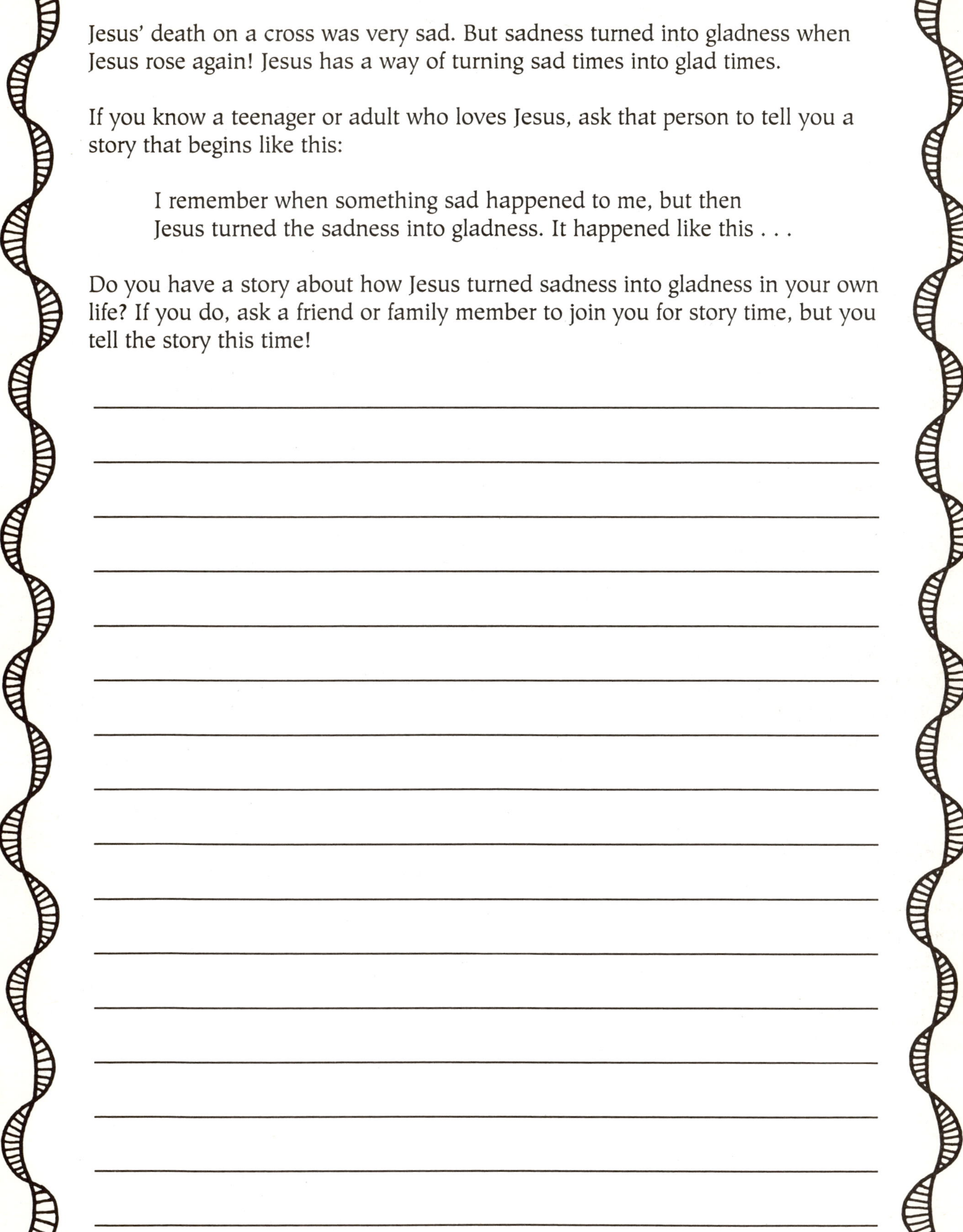

Jesus' death on a cross was very sad. But sadness turned into gladness when Jesus rose again! Jesus has a way of turning sad times into glad times.

If you know a teenager or adult who loves Jesus, ask that person to tell you a story that begins like this:

> I remember when something sad happened to me, but then Jesus turned the sadness into gladness. It happened like this . . .

Do you have a story about how Jesus turned sadness into gladness in your own life? If you do, ask a friend or family member to join you for story time, but you tell the story this time!

Watch for Signs of Jesus in Your Life

Luke 24:13–35

Cleopas jammed his few possessions into a bag. He was leaving Jerusalem—for good. All Jesus' miracles must have been magic tricks! In the end, Jesus couldn't even save himself from death on a cross.

"Grace!" Cleopas called to his 18-year-old daughter. "Hurry up! Emmaus is a full day's walk from here."

"Coming, Father!" she answered. Grace ran to keep up with Cleopas. "Why are you walking so fast? Are you upset?"

"You know why! Jesus is dead!" Cleopas kept marching.

"Yes, I know. But that makes me sad, not mad," Grace replied. "Why are you mad?"

Just then, a stranger joined Cleopas and Grace on the road. The traveler said, "Excuse me, what's going on? Everyone's acting so strange around here."

Cleopas snorted. But Grace patiently and tearfully told about Jesus' trial, death, and burial.

"Do you mind if I walk along with you?" the stranger asked.

Cleopas set the pace, so they walked fast. He said angrily, "I put all my hopes in Jesus. I thought he was the Son of God. But then he died. This morning, I got really confused. Some women went to Jesus' tomb, and it was empty! They said angels told them that Jesus is alive! Angels, mind you! Then some other friends went to the tomb. It was just as the women had said—no Jesus! I don't know what to believe."

The stranger squeezed the bridge of his nose, like he was trying not to get a headache.

"Don't you remember what the Scriptures say?" As they walked, the stranger talked about each place in Scripture that foretold what would happen to the Son of God. He pointed out how the events of Jesus' death fulfilled those Scriptures exactly.

When they reached Emmaus, Cleopas and Grace invited the traveler to eat supper with them. But when they sat down to eat, the traveler—not Cleopas—picked up the bread and said a blessing. When he broke the bread, Cleopas and Grace suddenly realized the man was Jesus! At that moment, the traveler disappeared.

Cleopas jumped up. "Hurry, Grace! Grab some bread to eat on the road. We're going back to Jerusalem tonight! We've got to spread the word that Jesus has risen from the dead— just as the Scriptures said!" This time, both Cleopas and Grace took off running.

Memory Verse
"And surely I am with you always, to the very end of the age" (Matthew 28:20b).

Why Did Jesus Appear This Way?
Why do you think Jesus didn't let Cleopas and Grace know who he was right away?

Prayer
Dear Jesus, thank you for being with me every minute of every day.

Look for Jesus in Your Life

Have you ever looked for signs of Jesus in your life? When you "see" Jesus today, it can be as exciting as when Cleopas and Grace saw Jesus on the road to Emmaus.

1. Look at yourself in a mirror. What do you see? Do you know that God formed every part of you and knew you before you were even born? God loves you just the way you are!

   Look in the mirror again. Do you see any scratches or scars? Even those can be reminders of how Jesus cared for you during a hard time.

2. Start a day with this prayer: Jesus, please let me see you in my life today.

   As you go through the day, watch for signs of Jesus. Did you pray a prayer that was answered? Was someone kind to you? Were you kind to someone else? All those things and more can be signs of Jesus in your life.

   At the end of the day, give thanks to Jesus for being in your life!

3. Keep a daily journal of where you see signs of Jesus.

IF9562 *Christian Virtues (Gr. 3–4)*

Listen to the Holy Spirit

Acts 8:26–38

Philip, one of Jesus' followers, was walking on a desert road. He was thinking about recent events—Jesus' triumphant ride into Jerusalem, his death on a cross, and the glorious day when Jesus rose again. He thought about how, after Jesus had gone up into heaven, he sent the Holy Spirit to live in his followers' hearts and minds.

"It's like having Jesus with me all the time—inside instead of outside!" thought Philip. "The Holy Spirit guides my life just as Jesus did when he was here. The Spirit helps me understand what God wants me to do."

Just then, a chariot approached Philip on the sandy road. The Holy Spirit urged Philip to go up to it. As it rolled toward Philip, he saw an officer of Ethiopia sitting behind the chariot driver. The man was reading aloud the words of God's prophet Isaiah. Running to keep up, Philip called out, "Do you understand what you're reading?"

"No! I need someone to explain it to me," replied the Ethiopian. He invited Philip to sit in the chariot with him. Philip saw what the man had been reading:

He was led like a sheep to the slaughter,
and as a lamb before the shearer is silent,
so he did not open his mouth.

The Ethiopian asked, "Who is the prophet talking about?" Philip explained that the passage foretold the death of Jesus. "Jesus?" asked the Ethiopian. "Isn't he the one who was crucified not so long ago?"

"Yes! Jesus' death took place just as Isaiah foretold!" replied Philip. As they rode, Philip told the Ethiopian about Jesus. "If you believe that Jesus is the Son of God, you can ask him to forgive your sins. Then he'll give you eternal life."

"Well, I can see that what's written is true. And I see something in you, Philip, that I don't see in others. I will ask Jesus to forgive me and come into my life." When the Ethiopian finished praying, he asked Philip, "What else shall I do?"

Philip answered, "When you're ready to show God and others that you're going to live by what you believe, you can be baptized."

The Ethiopian stood up, shading his eyes from the fierce sun. "Driver!" he shouted. "Stop by that water up there. I will be baptized now!"

The chariot stopped by a pool that bubbled up from an underground spring. Philip and the Ethiopian went down to the water. There, Philip baptized this new believer in Jesus Christ. As the Ethiopian rose up out of the water, Philip thought, "Now what started all this? Oh, yes! The Holy Spirit!"

Memory Verse
"The Holy Spirit, whom the Father will send in my name, will teach you all things and will remind you of everything I have said to you" (John 14:26).

How Did the Holy Spirit Talk to Philip?
How do you think Philip knew what the Holy Spirit was saying to him? How do you think people today can know what the Holy Spirit wants them to do?

Prayer
Dear God, thank you for sending the Holy Spirit to help me know what to do.

"Three-in-One" Experiment

God is sometimes called the great Three-in-One: God the Father, God the Son (Jesus), and God the Holy Spirit. This experiment can help you understand how God can be "Three-in-One."

1. Put four ice cubes in a small saucepan. What is ice?

2. With an adult's help, put the kettle on the stove and turn the burner to medium-high. Watch what happens to the ice. Now what do you have?

3. With an adult still helping you, let the water boil. What do you see in the air above the kettle?

Water was present in each of the three steps above, but in three different forms—ice, water, and steam.

A simple experiment like this can't fully explain God the Father, God the Son, and God the Holy Spirit. But it can help you understand how one God can be present in three forms.

Answer Key
1. *frozen* water   2. *liquid* water   3. steam, or *vaporized* water

---

Remember: God Can Make Big Changes!

Acts 9:1–6

Jesus. Oh, that name made Saul boiling mad! "People who believe in Jesus are nuts! They don't even deserve to live!" Saul kicked his horse in the ribs to go faster. He couldn't wait to get to Damascus. He was going to find every last one of those "Christians" and bring them back to Jerusalem as prisoners! He hoped they would all end up like Stephen—stoned to death for his beliefs. "Hah!" Saul threw his head back and laughed.

Suddenly, a bright light from heaven shot to the ground and knocked Saul right off his horse! Saul shook his head, dazed. Then something even scarier happened.

"Saul! Saul! Why do you persecute me?" rang out a voice from heaven.

"Wh . . . Who . . . are you, Lord?" stammered Saul.

"I am Jesus! The one you are persecuting!" The voice struck terror in Saul's heart. "Now get up and go into the city. Then I'll tell you what to do."

Saul staggered to his feet. His knees went weak. He fell dizzily to the side of the road. His heart pounded. His whole body shook. At last, Saul opened his eyes. He couldn't see! He was blind! Jesus had spoken. In an instant, Saul's life was forever changed.

The blindness lasted only a few days, but the changes in Saul's life lasted forever. In fact, before long he became known as Paul. He had a new name to go with his new life! The old Saul had done all he could to stop the Good News of Jesus Christ from spreading. But the new Paul dedicated every minute of his new life to that very Jesus. He carried the story of Jesus on his travels, sharing it with all who would listen.

Can Jesus make big changes in someone's life? You bet he can!

Memory Verse
"He rules forever by his power"
(Psalm 66:7a).

What Happened Next?
Read Acts 9:7–19 to discover how God restored Saul's eyesight.

Prayer
Dear God, thank you that with your power, you can change what seems impossible!

From Bug to Butterfly

Saul became a new person after he met Jesus. Saul even got a new name—Paul! This craft can remind you of the big, beautiful changes God can make in a person's life. With God, a bug can become a butterfly!

Bug

Materials:
five pom-pom balls strung together
two craft sticks
two plastic movable eyes
glue

Directions:

1. Glue a craft stick to the side of the first and last pom-pom on the string so that the craft stick hangs down.

2. Glue the eyes on one of the end pom-poms.

Now you have a bug puppet! You can make your bug crawl along a table edge or the back of a chair. But it can only crawl. To fly, it must become a butterfly.

Why be a bug when God can change you into a butterfly!

Butterfly

Materials:
tissue paper   markers
string or ribbon scissors
construction paper glue

Directions:

1. Fold a piece of tissue paper in half. On the fold, draw the outline of a butterfly wing, then cut it out. (Don't cut along the fold.) When you open your folded paper, you'll have a butterfly.

2. With markers, carefully color your tissue-paper butterfly.

3. Make a body for your butterfly out of construction paper.

4. Lay a piece of string across the center of your butterfly, then glue the body over the string.

5. Holding the ends of the string, bounce your hands up and down to make your butterfly fly.

Keep Your Heart Open to God's Message

Acts 16:11–15

Lydia! Do we have 10 bolts of purple cloth for the palace?"

"Lydia! The governor wants the finest purple for new robes!"

"Lydia! The judge's wife wants you to measure her windows for new purple drapes!"

That was yesterday. Today was the Sabbath, the day of rest. Lydia sat with some other women in the shade by the river, praying. Unlike the others, Lydia fidgeted as she prayed. She couldn't get the demands of everyday business off her mind. "Oops. I forgot to write down that rush order for Marcus." Lydia opened her eyes a crack, picked up a stick, and started writing a note to herself in the sandy soil. Suddenly, she saw a man's sandaled feet near her hand. She looked up. "What do you want? Who are you?" Lydia said.

The other women looked up, too, and saw several strangers standing near their group. These were big men—strong and rugged. They looked a little frightening.

The leader of the group said, "We wondered if we could talk with you. We noticed from your prayers that you believe in God."

Well, this guy looked tough, but he spoke quietly and politely. When he mentioned God, Lydia felt her heart stir. Her straying mind suddenly snapped to attention. She glanced at the other women, then said, "Yes. Join us. We want to hear what you have to say."

The man introduced himself as Paul. He told the good news about Jesus Christ's life, death, and resurrection. He explained how the women could have eternal life.

Lydia responded first. "God has opened my heart to your message. I believe what you say. I want to invite Jesus into my life and be baptized. But first, I want everyone in my house to hear about this, too." Lydia and some of the other women sent for their families and servants. When they arrived, Paul told them all the message of Jesus Christ, and they believed, too. Lydia stood up and brushed grass from her robe. "Well, there's no time like right now!" she said in her get-it-done way. "The river is a perfect place to be baptized!"

Paul baptized the new believers. Then Lydia announced, "Listen up, everyone. You'll all come to supper at my house tonight. Paul, you and your friends will stay in my guest quarters." Paul protested, not wanting to impose, but Lydia replied firmly, "No arguing!" And that was that.

Memory Verse
"The Lord opened her heart to respond to Paul's message" (Acts 16:14b).

What Would Lydia Be Like Today?
Lydia was a businesswoman who could make fast, good decisions, then act on them quickly. Do you know anyone who's a little like Lydia?

Prayer
Dear God, please help me keep an open heart to your message.

An Open Heart

This craft can help you keep your heart open to God's message.

1. Fold a piece of red or pink construction paper in half.
2. On the fold, draw half of a heart. With the paper still folded, cut out the heart.
3. Lay the heart on another piece of red or pink paper and cut around it, so you have two hearts the same size and shape. If you wish, you may also cut out several white hearts to insert between the colored hearts.
4. Lay one heart on top of the other heart. On the top heart, print the following words:

   My heart is open to God's message.

   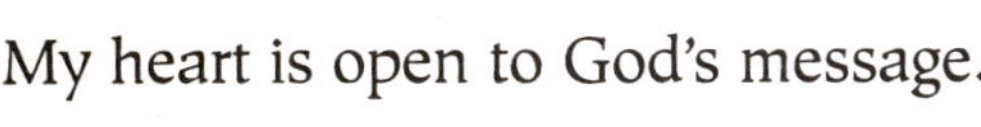

   Decorate the top heart, if you wish.
5. Staple the hearts together with two staples on the left side. Now you can open and close your heart like a book.

6. Inside your heart book, keep track of God's messages to you. For instance, if God answers a prayer you prayed, open your heart and write something like this:

   God answers my prayers.

   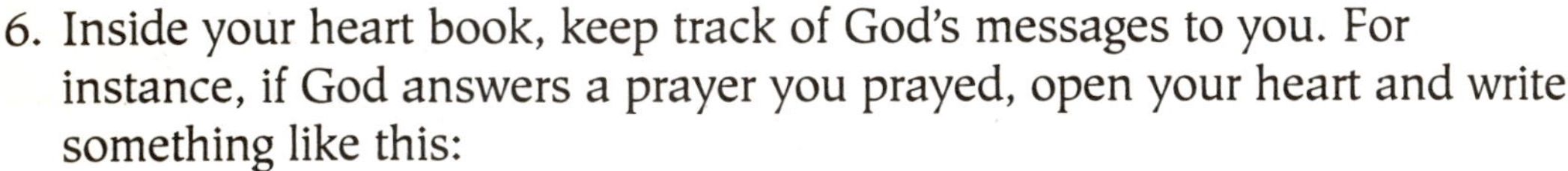

If you learn a lesson at church about God's love, open your heart when you get home and write something like this:

   God will always love me.

Soon, your heart will be filled with God's messages!

Let Jesus Shine Through Your Life

Acts 18:1–4, 18–28

"What a town!" thought Paul as he looked around Corinth. Paul saw exotic animals, spices, jewels, and slaves for sale in the city's market. "Hmm. What's this?" he wondered, peering into a large, dark shop.

"Can I help you?" a voice boomed out.

"What are you selling?" asked Paul.

"Tents," chimed a lighter, musical voice. "You tell us the size and color, and we'll make a tent like no other!"

"What do you know! I'm a tentmaker, too," said Paul.

"Glad to meet you," said the deep voice. "I'm Aquila, and this is my wife, Priscilla. What brings you to Corinth?"

Paul replied, "I'm here to spread the Good News about Jesus Christ."

"Well! That's exactly what we do as we go about our work every day," smiled Priscilla. "We just got a big order from the army for tents. Would you like to work with us?" Paul readily agreed. Over the next few weeks, the three talked about Jesus as they sewed the tents.

Every Sabbath, the three friends went to the synagogue to talk about the Scriptures and worship God. Priscilla and Aquila helped Paul reason with Corinth's leaders. The three friends explained that Jesus had fulfilled the Scripture's promise of a king. During the week, people often stopped by their shop to ask questions and talk more about Jesus.

After several months, the three tentmakers set sail for another city, Ephesus. They set up shop and went to the synagogue, just as they had in Corinth. When Paul left Ephesus, Aquila and Priscilla remained behind.

One day, Priscilla and Aquila heard a newcomer, Apollos, speak in the synagogue at Ephesus. Apollos knew the Scriptures well and even taught about Jesus. But Priscilla and Aquila could tell that Apollos hadn't heard that Jesus had died and rose again.

Aquila went up to Apollos. "We'd like to invite you to dinner, friend," he said. Over the meal, they discussed the whole story of Jesus! Then Apollos really began preaching the gospel—the whole gospel! As he traveled, he encouraged Christians and led many others to believe in Jesus.

Back in Ephesus, and in all their travels after that, Priscilla and Aquila kept making tents, making friends, and sharing the story of Jesus.

Memory Verse
"I am the light of the world. Whoever follows me will never walk in darkness, but will have the light of life" (John 8:12).

Were Priscilla and Aquila Tentmakers or Missionaries?

Priscilla and Aquila made a living by making tents. But they also told people about Jesus. Do you think they were tentmakers? missionaries? or both?

Prayer

Dear Jesus, thank you for being in my life. Please shine through me, so others can see you too.

Where Can Jesus Shine Through?

Jesus' love can shine through everything you do. On the chart below, make a list of 20 things you like to do. (That sounds like a long list, but once you get started, you'll probably think of even more than 20 things you like to do!) Then, look at your list carefully. Check each item where Jesus' love could shine through.

20 Things I Like to Do

1. ______________________________ ☐
2. ______________________________ ☐
3. ______________________________ ☐
4. ______________________________ ☐
5. ______________________________ ☐
6. ______________________________ ☐
7. ______________________________ ☐
8. ______________________________ ☐
9. ______________________________ ☐
10. ______________________________ ☐
11. ______________________________ ☐
12. ______________________________ ☐
13. ______________________________ ☐
14. ______________________________ ☐
15. ______________________________ ☐
16. ______________________________ ☐
17. ______________________________ ☐
18. ______________________________ ☐
19. ______________________________ ☐
20. ______________________________ ☐

Know How to Show Love to Others

1 Corinthians 13:1–13

Paul, we have another letter concerning the church at Corinth today," called Sosthenes as he ran up the stairs to Paul's room.

"Is there still trouble in Corinth?" Paul asked.

His friend replied, "Yes, I'm afraid so. The people there still want to live their own way instead of God's way. Here, read it for yourself."

Paul carried the letter to a chair by the window. After he read it, his eyes strayed to the dusty courtyard below. Children laughed and played a game with sticks and stones. Donkeys brayed for their dinner. Two of Paul's friends, Sharon and Deborah, cooked a pot of soup over an open fire. Paul heard the sisters arguing. "You just can't stay out of my business, can you, Sharon? You're always telling me what to do. Won't you ever let me grow up and make my own decisions?" complained Deborah.

Sharon smiled at Deborah. "You're my sister. I love you and want what's best for you. I'm not telling you what I want you to do. It's what God wants you to do," said Sharon.

Deborah snapped, "How do you know what God wants me to do?"

"You heard the Master's teaching. Jesus wants us to live a life that's pleasing to God," said Sharon. "God loves us and wants us to love one another."

Deborah replied, "Okay. I guess I can put up with your advice as long as it's for my own good!" The two sisters hugged.

Paul, listening from the window above, thought, "That's just what the people in Corinth need to know—how to love each other!" Paul grabbed his pen and began to write. He wrote all afternoon and into the evening. Sosthenes had brought his supper, but it had gone cold.

Sosthenes himself had fallen asleep with his head on Paul's lumpy pillow!

As the room brightened with the dawn, Paul put down his pen at last. He shook Sosthenes. "Wake up, my patient friend! I have much to tell you! God used you, Deborah, and Sharon to help me know what to say to the people at Corinth!" Paul rejoiced. "Look! Here's a small sample of what I wrote:

Love is patient and kind. Love isn't jealous or boastful. Love isn't rude. It doesn't anger easily. It doesn't keep a record of wrongs. Love never fails!

"Paul, your words are true and good. The people of Corinth need to hear them!" replied Sosthenes.

"Well, if you'll take this letter to a messenger right away, I'll close my eyes and get some sleep," said Paul. He took Sosthenes' place on the bed. Paul was asleep almost before his head hit the pillow.

Memory Verse
"Love is patient, love is kind"
(1 Corinthians 13:4a).

How Did Paul's Friends Help?
How did Sosthenes, Deborah, and Sharon help Paul to know what to write about love?

Prayer
Dear Jesus, help me to know how to show love to others.

Write a Love Letter

In Bible times, people didn't have telephones or e-mail. They used letters to communicate with each other. Today, letters are still a good way to send messages.

Do you know someone who needs to know about God's love? If you do, write your own "love" letter, just as Paul did! The sentence starters below can help you write your letter.

Dear

I'm so glad to have a chance to write you, because . . .

I'd like to share with you some lessons I've learned about God's love . . .

What do you think about all this? If you write me a letter back, I'll . . .

With love,

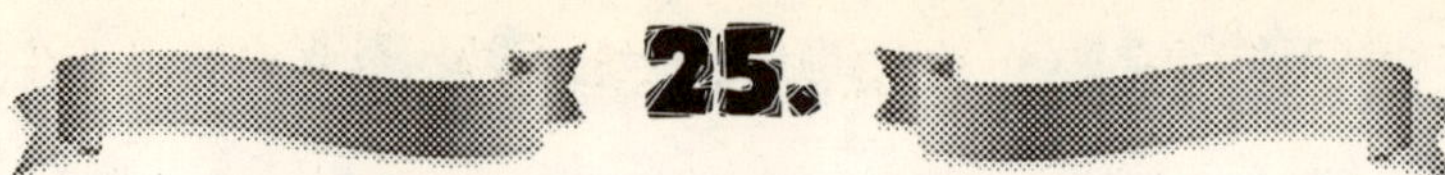

25.

Encourage Others to Live Godly Lives

2 Timothy 3:14–17

Timothy watched the ships sail in and out of the city of Ephesus. Seagulls flew overhead. Timothy heard them squawk as they tried to steal bits of fish from the fishing boats. As Timothy watched, he thought, "I hope one of these ships is bringing a letter from Paul."

"Timothy!" The young man turned at the sound of his name. "Timothy! It's here! The letter from Paul has arrived at last!" Timothy's friend Aquila waved a scroll in the air as he came running. Aquila handed the papers carefully to Timothy.

"Thank you, dear friend," said Timothy as he reached for the letter.

"Take your time reading the letter, Tim. Priscilla and I will keep some supper warm for you whenever you're ready to eat."

"Thanks, Aquila. I hope to be along soon," replied Timothy. He immediately sat down on a rock and began to read.

Paul had been like a father to Timothy. With Paul's help, Timothy had grown from a boy who knew Scripture to a man who lived for Jesus Christ.

"Well," Timothy thought, "I'll have to take time later to read this letter closely." Just then, some words seemed to jump right out of the letter: "Continue in what you have learned."

"Oh, Paul," Timothy whispered. "That is exactly what I needed to hear." Timothy looked out to sea and thought, "Sometimes it's so hard to live a Christian life. I get discouraged. Sometimes I want to give in and be like everybody else. Paul's words encourage me to keep on living a godly life. With God's help— and the support of friends like Paul—that's just what I'm going to do!"

> **Memory Verse**
> "Don't let anyone look down on you because you are young" (1 Timothy 4:12a).

Have You Ever Heard Encouraging Words?
Paul's words of encouragement helped Timothy. Has someone ever given you words of encouragement? If so, how did you feel after hearing those words?

Prayer
Dear Jesus, thank you for friends who encourage me. Please help me to remember to encourage others.

Encourage Someone You Love

On the chart below, make a list of the people you love. Next to each name, write something that is a challenge or is difficult for that person. Then, for each person, write some encouraging words on a slip of paper (see the example below). Tuck the paper into a sock drawer, a lunch bag, a briefcase, or anyplace that will surprise the person who finds it. Remember—an encouraging word can let someone know you care, even when you're not there.

People I love	Something that is a challenge
Example: *Big sister*	*Example:* *Learning to drive a car*
1.	
2.	
3.	
4.	
5.	
6.	

Encouraging Words
Hey, big sis! I'll pray for you during your driving lesson today. Keep God in the driver's seat, and you'll do just fine!

Always Wear God's Invisible Armor

Ephesians 6:13–18

It was a warm, sunny day in the city of Ephesus. Jed was on his father's boat, helping his dad fix a broken sail. Jed pulled the heavy canvas tight as his dad sewed with strong cord. Jed asked, "Where did you go last night, Dad?"

"Ha! So you've been keeping an eye on me, have you, son?" Jed's dad teased. Jed grinned back.

"I was meeting with some Christian friends, Jed," Dad explained. "Last week, Paul sent a letter to the Christians here in Ephesus. We're sending the letter around to all the Christian groups in the city. Last night was our group's turn to read it."

Jed's ears perked up. He had met Paul before. "What did Paul have to say?" Jed asked.

"Oh, it was just something about a soldier's armor. You know, kind of boring," Jed's dad said with a twinkle in his eye.

Jed sat up straight and exclaimed, "A soldier's armor! You mean like the armor I made for my toy soldier? Tell me about it!"

Jed's dad laughed. "Okay, I'll tell you what Paul said. But first, you tell me why soldiers wear armor."

"Well," Jed began, "armor protects soldiers from swords and spears."

"That's right," said Dad. "Paul said a Christian needs armor, too. We need protection from sharp words and attacks. What are the parts of armor you made for your soldier, Jed?"

"Well, I made a belt, a breastplate, special shoes, a shield, a helmet, and . . . and . . . oh, yeah—a sword."

"That's exactly the kind of armor Paul talked about!" said Jed's dad.

"You mean I'm going to have to wear heavy armor?" Jed asked.

"No. God's armor is invisible! Imagine yourself dressed in a belt made of truth—the truth we know from Jesus. Your invisible breastplate is righteousness—the moral way Jesus wants you to live. Your shoes guide your steps in the gospel of peace. Your shield is your faith that you hold out in front of you. See what I mean?"

"Yeah. But what about the rest of the armor?" asked Jed.

"Your helmet is salvation—it gives you eternal life. And your sword is the sword of the Spirit—the Word of God!"

Jed closed his eyes and imagined himself dressed in the armor of God. "With God's armor, I can face anything!" he said.

Memory Verse
"Put on the full armor of God, so that . . . you may be able to stand your ground" (Ephesians 6:13).

Do You Need Armor Today?
Paul wrote about God's armor hundreds of years ago. Do you think Christians still need God's armor today? Why, or why not?

Prayer
Dear God, thank you that you give us the protection we need when the going gets rough.

Dress in God's Armor

Copy or trace and color the pieces of armor below. Trace or copy the figure of the person, then color it to look like you. Cut out all the pieces. Now dress yourself in the armor of God!

Belt of Truth

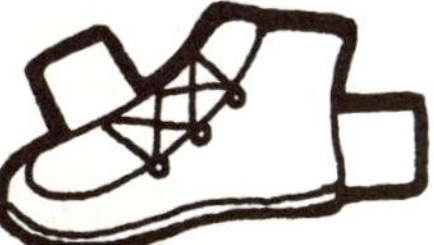 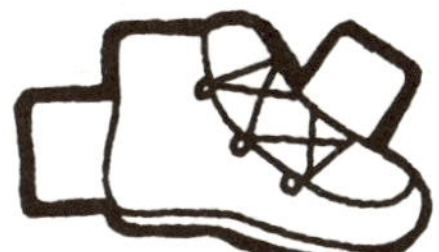

Shoes of Peace

Breastplate of Righteousness

Shield of Faith

Helmet of Salvation

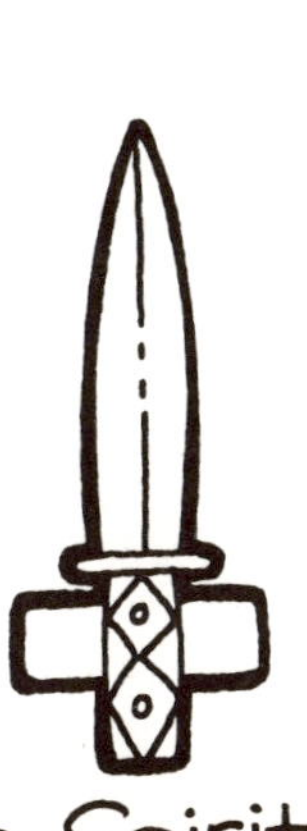

Sword of the Spirit

Let the Fruit of the Spirit Grow in Your Life

Galatians 5:22–26

Paul lit the fire outside his tent. As the flames grew, he warmed his hands with the fire's heat. Paul's friend Joab was asleep in the tent. Paul chuckled as he heard Joab snore. "That will keep the wild animals away!" thought Paul. He and Joab had stopped for the night on their journey to Jerusalem. But Paul couldn't sleep.

Paul was concerned about the people of Galatia. When Paul had preached God's Word to them, they cheered and clapped. They shouted "Yes!" and "Amen!" But when Paul left Galatia to spread God's Word in other places, the people forgot how God wanted them to live.

Paul knew he had to write the Galatians a letter. He pulled his cloak tighter around him and threw some wood on the fire. Paul pulled his knees up as he sat, then laid his head down on his folded arms. "Oh, Lord," he prayed, "give me the right words to say to the people of Galatia."

Paul reached into his pack for something to write with. Feeling around in the pack, Paul's hand touched some plump figs he'd picked from the tree in Joab's yard. As Paul bit into the sweet fruit, he remembered the fig tree that produced the fruit. Everyone who passed by Joab's tree marveled at all the fruit that hung from its branches. Thoughtfully, Paul began to write.

At morning's first light, Joab peeked out of the tent. He saw Paul curled up by the cold fire, his hand resting on the letter he'd written. Joab read: "But the fruit of the Spirit is love, joy, peace, patience, kindness, goodness, faithfulness, gentleness and self-control."

Paul rubbed his eyes and sat up. Joab said, "Paul! This is it! This is exactly what the people in Galatia need to hear! You've told them what their lives will look like when they live by faith."

"So, Joab, you think it gets the idea across?" Paul asked groggily.

"Yes! But what made you think of fruit?" Joab asked.

"Well," Paul began with a smile, "it was the sweet taste of that fruit from your healthy fig tree!" laughed Paul.

"Did you eat all those figs? I wanted one for breakfast!" teased Joab. "I should have stayed up to guard those figs last night!"

Paul replied, "Well, at least that would have kept you from snoring!"

Memory Verse
"Let us do good to all people"
(Galatians 6:10).

Are You Bearing Fruit?
Think about the fruit of the Spirit—love, joy, peace, patience, kindness, goodness, faithfulness, gentleness, and self-control. Do you have any of these fruit growing on your "tree"?

Prayer
Dear God, please help the fruit of the Spirit grow in my life.

Fruit-of-the-Spirit Centerpiece

Materials:

a pretty bowl
9 pieces of fruit
9 toothpicks
9 small pieces of paper, the size of sticky notes

scissors
pen
tape

Directions:

On the small pieces of paper, write these words (one word per paper):

Love
Joy
Peace
Patience
Kindness

Goodness
Faithfulness
Gentleness
Self-Control

Tape each paper to a toothpick, so that it looks like a tiny flag. Arrange the pieces of fruit in a bowl. Stick one "flag" into each piece of fruit. Place the bowl on a table as a centerpiece. At a meal, ask these questions to see what your family has to say about the "fruit of the Spirit."

1. What are the "fruit of the Spirit"?
2. If your life is like a tree, how can you get the fruit of the Spirit to grow on it?
3. Do you have any fruit of the Spirit growing in your life now? Which one(s)?
4. Which fruit of the Spirit would you like to grow bigger and sweeter in your life?

28.
Watch Your Tongue!

James 3:3-12

James, where are you?" shouted Sharon from the kitchen. She looked out the window. Her husband sat in the shade of their stable, writing. "Is that all he cares about?" she wondered.

James did not hear Sharon call. He gave all his attention to the letter he was writing to the Jewish Christians. As a church leader in Jerusalem, James was giving them some advice.

Sharon put her hands on her hips and headed for James. Her feet kicked up little dust clouds. James didn't notice when Sharon stomped her foot and said, "Hmph!" Finally, Sharon said loudly, "James! I want to talk to you!"

James looked up. "Uh-oh," he thought. "Here comes a lecture."

Sure enough, Sharon scolded James for ignoring his daily chores. "I just want you to know that I'm tired of all your daydreaming and writing. I can't do all the work around here!"

James reached up and took his wife's hand. "You're right. I haven't done my share of the work today. But would you sit by me for just a minute?"

"Well, this had better be important," she said as she sat down next to her husband.

"I'm writing a letter to Jewish believers," said James. "I need to tell them to watch what they say. The tongue can be a powerful weapon. Here, see what I've written."

Sharon glanced at the paper James handed her. He had pointed out that a tiny bit in the mouth of a huge horse could control the whole animal. He also wrote about how a small rudder steered a large ship. Finally, she said, "I think people who read this will understand that although the tongue is a small part of the body, it can cause big problems."

Sharon sat still for a minute. "James, did you write this letter to me? Are you preaching to me again?"

"No, no!" laughed James. "This letter is for everyone! Our tongues are always getting us into trouble and hurting other people's feelings. If we want to be more like Jesus, we should speak as he would speak."

"You mean we should learn to control our tongues?" asked Sharon.

"Yes," answered James. "We should think first and speak second. If our hearts are right with God, our tongues will speak words that please him."

Sharon touched James' arm. "I'm sorry I spoke harsh words to you."

"I'm sorry I made you angry," James said. "When I finish this letter, I'll do my chores and some of yours, too. I promise."

"That's okay. Take all the time you need to do God's work," Sharon said. "This letter will help many people."

Memory Verse
"Likewise the tongue is a small part of the body, but it makes great boasts"
(James 3:5a).

What Else Did James Write?

Read James 3:1–12 to see what else James had to say about controlling the tongue.

Prayer

Dear Jesus, please help me to control my tongue. Help me to think before I speak and to speak in ways that please you.

Tongue Tamers

Most people could use some practice taming their tongues! What would you say in these situations? Remember to think before you speak, and tame that tongue!

What would you say if . . .

you didn't like what was served for dinner? _______________________

____

____

you found out a friend told a lie about you? _______________________

____

____

a classmate shoved you on the playground? _______________________

____

____

your big brother or sister bossed you around? _______________________

____

____

someone called you a nasty name? _______________________

____

____

Extra!
Can you name some other situations where you might need to tame your tongue?

If You Make a Mistake, Set It Right

Philemon 8–18

Onesimus hid in a dark alley, hoping no one would see him. It was dangerous to be out. Onesimus was a runaway slave and wanted by the law. He slipped around the corner of a building and stopped to catch his breath. He wiped sweat from his forehead and prayed, "Dear Jesus, because of your teachings I know I have sinned. It was wrong to run away from my master. But now, if I go back, he has the right to kill me! Even if he forgives me, by law he can brand a big F on my forehead for being a fugitive—a runaway.

"I'm scared, Jesus. But I've decided to do the right thing anyway. Please help me," finished Onesimus.

The runaway slave took a deep breath and stepped out into the sunlight. "Before I leave town," he thought, "I'll make one last visit to Paul."

To visit Paul, Onesimus had to go to the jail. The famous teacher had been thrown in prison for speaking out about Jesus. "Jail!" Onesimus shook his head. "Dear Jesus, there will be a lot of soldiers in and around the jail. Please protect me!"

Onesimus arrived safely at the jail and was soon face to face with Paul. Heavy iron bars separated the two friends. Onesimus told Paul that he had decided to return to his master and ask forgiveness for running away.

Paul said, "You are brave, friend. You could die for this, you know."

Onesimus said, "Yes, I know."

"Hmm," said Paul. "Your master, Philemon, is an old friend of mine. He's also a believer in Christ. Maybe I can help you."

Paul sat down and began writing a letter to Philemon. Onesimus could read a few of the words: "I appeal to you for my son Onesimus . . . welcome him as you would welcome me. If he has done you any wrong or owes you anything, charge it to me" (Philemon 10, 17–18).

As Paul signed the letter, he said, "I will send this letter on ahead of you. My prayers and my love go with you. Have faith. You are doing the right thing."

"My dear, dear brother," Onesimus reached through the bars and clasped Paul's hand. "I never thought a slave and an important man like you could be friends. Now I know that all things are possible with God. I can trust God with my future."

Memory Verse
"With God all things are possible"
(Matthew 19:26b).

What Happened Next?
You can read all of Paul's letter to Philemon in the Bible. What do you think Philemon did when Onesimus, his runaway slave, returned?

Prayer
Dear Jesus, help me know when I make a mistake, and give me the courage to set things right again. Thank you that with you all things are possible.

PBPWMGINFWMY!

Can you read the word above? Of course not! It's not really a word. In this case, the letters stand for:

Please Be Patient With Me, God Is Not Finished With Me Yet!

Remember this saying when you make a mistake. It will remind you that God doesn't expect you to be perfect, but to keep trying to be more like Jesus. Make a poster with the words above to hang in your room. Decorate it however you'd like.

30

Look Forward to Seeing Jesus

Revelation 1:9–19

Bang! Bam! Clunk. John chipped away a rock that rolled down the hill and joined the increasingly larger pile of other rocks. "My arms are so sore," thought John. "I'm tired and thirsty, and I don't know how long I can keep this up."

John was a prisoner on the island of Patmos. Very few people ever returned from this hot, rocky island. The Roman soldiers simply worked the prisoners to death. John had been arrested and sent here because he preached about Jesus.

"The guard is leaving," John noticed. "Maybe I can rest a minute." John closed his eyes. As always, his mind went right to Jesus. Thinking about the loving kindness of the Son of God always refreshed John.

But this time when John closed his eyes, it seemed as if they opened again, only in a dream. A loud voice said to John, "Write on a scroll what you see, and send it to the seven churches."

John turned to look at the voice, and he saw someone "dressed in a robe . . . with a golden sash around his chest. His head and hair were . . . white as snow, and his eyes were like blazing fire. . . . his voice was like the sound of rushing waters. . . . His face was like the sun shining in all its brilliance" (Rev. 1:13–16).

In his dream, John fell to the ground. It was Jesus standing there! Jesus talked to John and showed him many things that he didn't understand. But, as Jesus commanded, John wrote down everything he saw and heard.

"Hey! Over there! Wake up!" John flinched as a rock hit him on the shoulder. "Get busy!" called the guard.

John stumbled to his feet and shook his head. What had happened? "I saw Jesus!" John remembered. Then he looked down at his hands. They weren't holding the rock-chipping tools. They were holding a scroll!

John carefully unrolled the scroll. One sentence seemed to jump off the page. It sent joy through John's aching, tired body: "Behold, I am coming soon!"

"Jesus said that!" whispered John. "I saw Jesus! And he's coming back!" John quickly stashed the scroll under some rocks for safekeeping. He began working with new energy. Lifting his head to the sky, John shouted, "I'm free! Nothing can hurt me, as long as I'm going to see Jesus again!"

Memory Verse
"Behold, I am coming soon! . . . Yes, I am coming soon" (Revelation 22:7a, 20b).

What Happened to John's Scroll?
The words John wrote on his scroll were read by Christians in the early church. You can read them today in the Book of Revelation.

Prayer
Dear Jesus, thank you for keeping all your promises. I'm looking forward to seeing you someday.

Ever-Ready

Do you know when Jesus is coming back? Of course not, no one knows! That means Christians need to be ready at all times to meet Jesus! Use the directions below to make a clock to remind yourself to be ever-ready to meet Jesus.

1. Around the rim of a paper plate, write the numbers 1 through 12, as you'd see them on a clock.
2. Inside the curve of the numbers, write: Be Ever-Ready to Meet Jesus!
3. Cut out "hands" for the clock from posterboard or cardboard.
4. Attach the hands to the clock with a metal fastener.
5. Whenever you look at the clock, remember that Jesus is coming back!

Notes

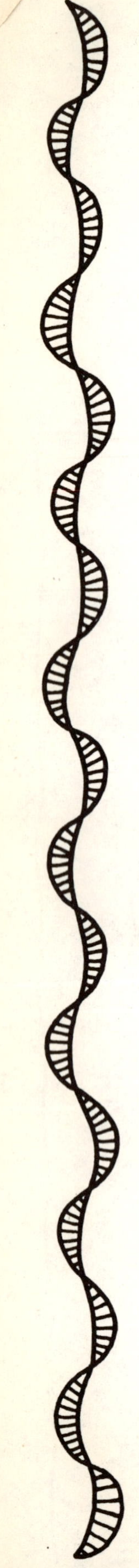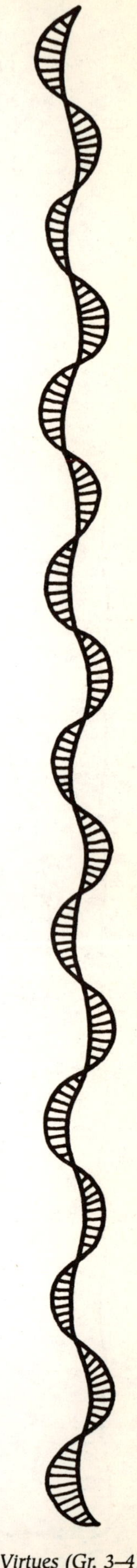

IF9562 *Christian Virtues (Gr. 3–4)*